ISOBEL,
WITH LOVE
GRANDMA

A
UST 14

Confidence for Kids By Kids

Written by

Class 4, Lambley Primary School

& Lisa Spencer-Arnell

First published in Great Britain

All paper used in the printing of this book has been made from wood grown in managed, sustainable forests.

ISBN13: 978-1-78003-737-0

Printed and bound in the UK
Pen Press is an imprint of
Indepenpress Publishing Limited
25 Eastern Place
Brighton
BN2 1GJ

Printed and bound in the UK by Orbital Print Ltd
www.orbitalprint.co.uk

A catalogue record of this book is available from the British Library

Cover design by Sarah Morley,
Originally based on a design by Aimee Hogg,
Adapted for publication by Jacqueline Abromeit.

Dedicated to:

All the Children in the World

Be who you are, believe in yourself,
you are worth it!

Acknowledgements

We'd like to say thank you to everyone who helped us put the book together and to those who shared their wisdom and personal stories on the importance of having good self belief to live a happy, successful life.

A BIG Thank You to Richard Branson, Stuart Pearce, 10 Downing Street, Billy Schwer, Sian Williams, Kerensa Jennings, Rory Delap, Gary Bailey, Emma Clayton, David Wood and Gareth Evans for all your wise words.

We'd like to acknowledge & thank Michael Wisher, Nottingham businessman and charity supporter, for sponsoring our project and enabling it to come to the attention of millions.

Special thanks to those who made pulling this book together possible, through giving their time, their services or connecting us with other people. We'd like to mention:-

Glynn at Wow Designs for creating and hosting our website.
(www.wowdesignsolutions.com)
(www.confidenceforkidsbykids.com)

Sarah Morley for pulling the design together for our cover.
(www.designforaday.co.uk)

Nicky Regan at Creative Dynamic Print for her sterling efforts in getting the first edition of the book printed so speedily.
(www. creativedynamicprint.co.uk)
And Lynn & Elizabeth at Indepenpress for pulling things together and publishing our book.
(www.Indepenpress.co.uk)

Jo Welch for taking the beautiful photos of the children.
(www.jokatywelch.com – Artist & Photographer)

Stephen Poulton for formatting our book so brilliantly.
(mobile: 07855 2244149 – Graphic Designer)

Tyna Burnett for sharing her version of a story.
(www.holisticalliance.co.uk)

Thanks a million Jo Simpson, Chris Moss, Rob Ansell, Kerensa Jennings, Kristy Ryan, Sue Stone, Louise Third and Sue Cokayne for your gift of contacting and connecting.

Contents

Why We Wrote This Book

We believe that self belief, self esteem and confidence are really important in helping us do whatever we want to do in life. It could be to help us with our exams, to try something new, to help deal with difficult situations and later on in life it'll help us with our qualifications and to get a job. All in all we think it's a very good reason to spend time on it. So we decided to give other kids some tips on how to be more confident in different situations and we hope it will help children everywhere.

We also want to raise money for a good charity and after lots of discussion in class, we decided to give the profits from this book to ChildLine, a fantastic charity which helps children like us, who need help with bullying or other problems. We hope to raise lots of money through the sales of this book, so please tell other people about it.

About The Authors

We the authors of this book are a class of 24 ten and eleven year old children from Lambley Primary School in Nottingham.

We are:-

Grace Arnell, Izaak Arnold, Oliver Bordino, Henry Brooks, Thomas Buggy, Michael Everton, Oliver Frammingham, JJ Hylton, Charlie Hines, Aimee Hogg, Oliver Ingram, Rio Joseph, Jess Machin, Luke Mitchell, Syme Mulvany, Adam Perry, Poppy Prince, Honey Rich, Millie Robertson-James, Mitchell Ryan, Joseph Sharp, Ali-Khan Somani, Caitlan Smeaton, Ellie Smith.

We wrote it together with Lisa Spencer-Arnell, one of the mums who is an author herself.

A Word From Lisa Spencer-Arnell

Thank you for picking up this book and reading it. The stars of this book really are the children. It's been a great project to work on with the children of class 4 and they've really put their heart and soul into it. The children decided what situations children needed more confidence in, what the tips are, what personal stories to share and importantly they chose the charity they wanted the profits of this book to be for, ChildLine. My role was to merely facilitate the book and get it in print. It's a fantastic achievement for the children to be published authors by the time they leave primary school and my hope is that it's helped with their confidence too. Our aim is to help other children around the world build their self belief and raise money for a great cause in the process.

The Little Diamond

Early one Saturday morning, a little diamond wakes up and says to himself, 'what a lovely day it is, I think I'll go for a walk.' So he decides he'll take a little stroll down the country lane of life. He gets ready and puts on his best training shoes, tying double knots just to make sure he doesn't trip up. As he leaves the house, he picks up the keys from the hall table, looks in the mirror and smiles to himself. He even gets a bling from his own bright reflection.

As he sets off, with the birds singing, and the butterflies fluttering by, he can hear the whirring noises of the farmer's machines behind the tall hedges either side of the lane. They're about to fertilise the ground ready to grow crops for the autumn. As the little diamond, walks along, he hears a plop plop noise and thinks to himself 'it must be raining,' but he can't see or feel any rain. He carries on walking, noticing the rabbits weaving in and out, feeling very happy with life and hears some more plop plop noises as he goes. With no sign of rain but more plop plop sounds, he just ignores it and carries on walking for an hour or so, until he starts to feel quite tired and heavy. 'Back home for a rest and a cup of tea' he decides. He sees some of his neighbours as he's walking down his road, and he waves, but they just laugh and walk by.

He finally turns the key in his shiny front door and walks through it with a heavy sigh. 'I'm feeling so tired now it's definitely time for a rest' and with that he puts his keys back on the hall table. As he does so, he catches a glimpse of himself in the mirror and steps back in shock. 'What! Can't be!' he thinks to himself, and takes another look. 'I must have had too much sun or.... Can't be the sun.' When he looks again he's horrified and realises he isn't a diamond after all, he's a lump of brown muck!

He sits down on the stairs and starts to cry; 'no-one will want to know me, no-one will talk to me, they'll think if they get too close to me they'll end up brown too'. He feels very sorry for himself and wonders what he can do. Suddenly he has an idea and gets his coat on, pulling his hood up very tight and goes off to the shops.

He keeps his head down so no-one sees him and goes into the supermarket to buy 30 bottles of the brightest shiniest red nail varnish he can find. He goes up to the counter to pay for it, still with his head down and the lady at the check-out thinks how very rude he is.

He runs home as fast as he can and he starts to paint himself. He paints and paints and he paints some more until he is completely covered in red shiny nail varnish. It takes him hours to cover every bit of brown, but when he takes another look in the mirror he feels so much better.

'People will like me now, they'll think I'm cool to be around, they'll want to hang out with me'. Then he has a thought, 'what if they hug me and it cracks', so he paints himself some more.

With a final look in the mirror he smiles and feels better, hoping that he'll be accepted and liked by people. He also feels a little bit sad that he's not who he thought he was, a diamond.

You see, the sad thing is, it wasn't his brown stuff at all, it was the farmers. But our little diamond took it on as his own. He so wanted to fit in that he painted himself, in the hope that people would like him more. If you take on other peoples brown stuff and put nail varnish on top, you're going to give the world a false impression of who you really are.

So here's the thing, if you ever find yourself in this position, I'm going to give you an invisible tool box. If you open the lid of the box, inside there's some forever clean cotton wool and never ending nail varnish remover, a brillo pad to scrub off the brown stuff and then there's a piece of beautiful plush purple velvet– a polishing cloth.

No matter what anyone says or tries to do, always remember you're a diamond. In fact always remember to polish your diamond, and don't wait for someone else to do it.

Occasionally one of the facets may be a little misty or faded. That's the time you say, "I'm no good at maths", "I can't do my homework", "I'm no good at sport" and that's when you spend some time polishing your diamond.

THE most important thing is that you never let anyone cover up your brilliance! Every child, every grown up is different and unique and has their own special gifts and strengths. Be who you are and everything else will follow!

Story Adapted by Tyna Burnett (www.holisticalliance.co.uk)

Confidence for Kids By Kids

What is confidence?

Confidence is about boldness, being sure you can do something, it's about your bravery. Confident people believe in themselves. It is very important to be confident because then you can do anything. When you are not confident you become nervous and that stops you doing things. Confidence is a good feeling, an expression, it makes you determined. When you're confident you stand up for yourself.

Why is confidence important?

Simple really, if you think you can you can, if you think you can't you won't. It's important so you're not scared. Without confidence you might get worse at something, you might lose hope and become nervous. With confidence you can do more. It helps you become stronger through life. So you can get on with anything. Confidence helps you do many things. Without confidence you won't be able to reach your highest standard.

What's the difference between self-confidence & self-esteem?

Self esteem is what you say about yourself inside and it's how you feel about you. Self confidence is what you feel about your own abilities, it's about what you do. It's important to like and accept yourself. Don't wait for other people to say you're ok, you are anyway. People can be confident and have low self esteem which is a shame. If you're good at things but don't like yourself much, then life feels like hard work. **Step 1** accept and like yourself. **Step 2** Practice and get better at doing things.

What (if anything) ever stops you from being more confident?

If someone is bullying you, it will knock you and your confidence. Getting hurt or trying something for the first time and not succeeding is hard. Seeing other people do better than you can get you down. Me saying negative things about myself stops me being more confident. But if I have good self esteem and I respect myself, then I deal with things better.

Here's when we think kids, like us, need more confidence:

With ourselves (our self esteem again)

At school

Doing sport

When things go wrong

With our family

When we're doing something new with our friends

When we have fears, phobias, or are nervous

Taking part in competitions, shows, presentations & demonstrations

With Ourselves

When we feel OK about ourselves, it's easier to be more confident and have a go at things.

Here are some things you can try:

Be yourself

When you start school and make friends, don't act like someone else be yourself. When I was in class 2, I was playing with my friends and they started talking about them growing up more and then I started to act tough and lady like. They were surprised and thought Millie never acts like that, what's she doing? It didn't feel good inside because I wasn't being myself. It's much easier when you're being yourself!

Millie, age 11

Be your own best friend

You've always got a friend, someone who cares for you. Some people may not like you or fall out with you at times, but there's always someone who likes you and that's your own best friend. I didn't want to leave my mum to start school. She had been always there for me and I was always stuck to her side. But when I went into my class there was this lovely teacher called Mrs Downes, and she welcomed me and I had fruit and milk with the class. I didn't know anybody and even though everyone was smiling, I wasn't sure if they would like me or not. It helped a bit that I have my own best friend- me!

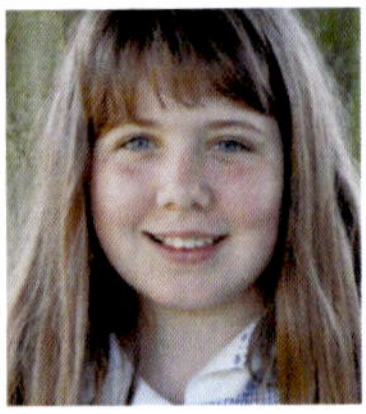

Grace, age 10

Be kind when you talk to yourself

I had a guitar exam and they said you've got 15 minutes to practice and then you're going to go in. In the practice I forgot everything, I was shouting at myself saying I can't do it. That didn't make me feel better at all, so I relaxed and was kinder to myself. In the end I went in, passed the test and got a distinction.

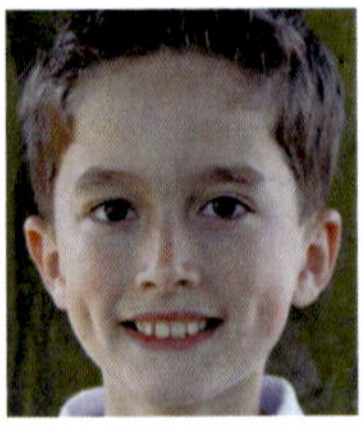

Oliver B, age 10

When someone says something good to you, remember it

A few years ago I was helping some little kids reading and the teacher thanked me and she said to me that "you were really helpful". She noticed I helped the children break down the words and said how much that helped them. It made me feel happy to think that I'd helped someone out and that might help them in their life. I still think about that sometimes, especially when I'm reading or helping my sister to read. It makes me feel good.

Millie, age 11

Focus on who you are and what you're good at, not what you can't do

If you're trying to do something you're not really good at and people keep on telling you to do it, don't bother. It doesn't really matter if you're not as good at that as those people. You're going to be good at something. I like to play football because I enjoy it and I'm good at it. I don't really keep on doing stuff I don't really like to do, like skipping. I'm not a natural skipper so I don't do it on a daily basis. It's hard because I see lots of other people skipping but I stick to the things I like doing. I like sport though I'm not amazing at them all but it's important that I enjoy it and have fun. If you keep doing something you can get better and better. Practise makes perfect. If you do something you hate, you'll never get good at it. If you don't like what you're doing, what's the point?

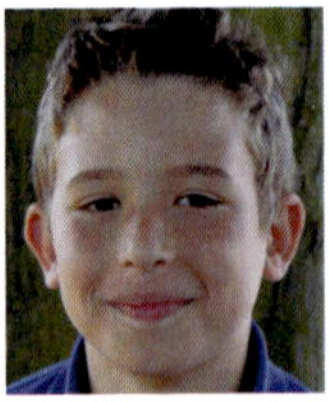

Rio, age 10

Hold your head high

There's nothing wrong with you even if you have a disability, everyone should be treated the same even if you're different. Different is good and most people are different. When I started the school I was different because I had a different accent to everyone else. People asked questions about where I was from. I felt proud that I was different.

Caitlan, age 11

Blank other people out, when you're trying to concentrate

I play golf and I've got a tournament coming up soon. My coach says it doesn't matter if I miss and he says don't get too nervous and just think back to when I hit balls on the range. I play with year 8s and 10s and that makes me feel nervous on club nights. When I play in the tournament I'm going to blank everyone out and imagine I'm playing on my own which will take the nerves away.

Thomas B, age 11

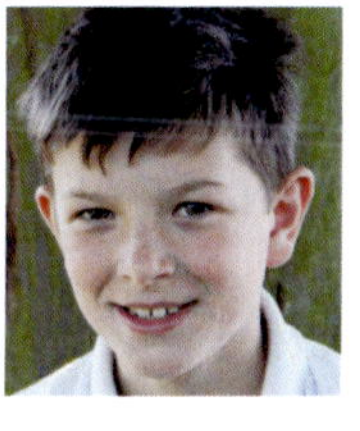

Say to yourself keep going, don't give up

I was in my Nottingham High School exam and I was absolutely trembling with fear of failing and I kept on thinking; 'I can't do it, I just can't do it.' Later on though, I realised it wasn't as hard as I thought it would be and I eventually found the courage to say to myself, just keep going and you will do fine. I finally went on with the exam with courage and the hope that I would pass. In the end I think I did alright, apart from maybe a few mistakes here and there, and as I walked away into the entrance hall I thought to myself, I might just have passed.

Mitchell, age 11

Happiness is the key – remember happy times and good things that have happened

When I was in class 1, my friend left me out and I felt really lonely and sad. Sometimes I wondered why she did it. As I sat on my own, I remembered myself and that I'm my own friend, which made me feel much better. I also thought about the holiday I'd been on with my family and that made me smile. I went and asked another friend Millie if I could play with her, she said yes and that inspired me to be more confident in myself and make sure other people aren't left out.

Grace, age 10

Compare you with you – don't compare yourself with other people

In class we were doing art and we had to draw a William Morris picture. I looked over at my friend's picture and thought it was really good. So I rubbed my work out and copied off her. I had several attempts at doing this and none of them were quite right but the first picture I did was actually better than any of my attempts to copy. So I learnt, never to copy off my friends, even if I think anything they've done is better than my version. It's far better to compare me with me.

Ellie, age 10

ACTIVITY 1

What's good about being you? Write a list of 10 positive statements about you, that start with "I am..."

1. I am ....

2. I am ....

3. I am ....

4. I am ....

5. I am ....

6. I am ....

7. I am ....

8. I am ....

9. I am ....

10. I am ....

TIP: If you want to grow your list, ask people you care about and trust what they value about you.

Keep adding to this list and read it often.

At School

When you go to school, you are with lots of different people. You make new friends, and get on with some people, maybe not with everyone. Being confident makes life at school easier.

Here's how:

Do your best

Maths and art are not my best subjects at school but I still have a go at them. I didn't used to like division but because I've tried my best, I now find it easy. Sometimes you just have to guess the answer but always remember to just try your best.

Poppy, age 10

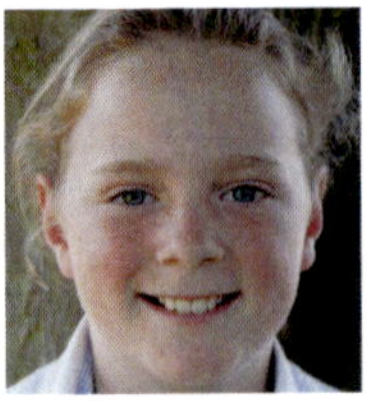

Always ask for help, if you're struggling

In my maths lesson, we were doing timetables and we had to find out what time programmes came on. I was struggling with it and I kept trying to do it, but got it wrong several times. I couldn't do it on my own so I had to ask the teacher. I felt much better after she helped me and then I didn't need to get help anymore.

Honey, age 11

Relax with your exams

Last week we were doing practice SATS and we had to figure out all the questions. I thought I'd got most of them wrong and out of 50 I got 37 so I got more than half right and got more than I thought I would. The reason was because I'd relaxed a bit. I was rushing when I first did it but I told myself that I could do it and to slow down. That helped a lot.

Millie, age 11

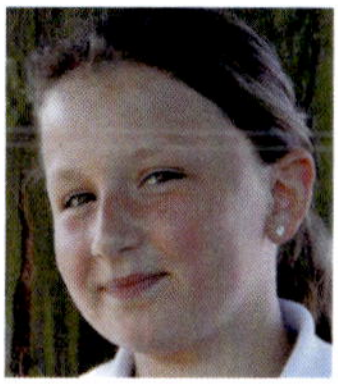

Speak with your teachers

Last year my friends and I fell out and I thought it would never be put right. We kept walking away from each other every day and no-one was talking. Eventually I decided that I'd had enough and I went to tell the teacher. I told her what had happened and she brought everyone together. We all talked to each other again and everyone apologised. Then the next day we were friends again and I felt a lot happier.

Aimee, age 11

Be positive – expect the best

We were in the finals of the small schools George Abbots Shield. We didn't know the opposition but we knew it was going to be a tough match. Personally I thought we were going to lose but I put that out of my mind and focussed on the match, making sure I thought we could win it. It was a scorching hot day. Two minutes before we started we had a team talk about the hard match we were about to play. Our Coach Mick said "it's a hot day and we need to think positive, if we lose a goal don't put your heads down, and you can win this. I believe in you". The whistle blew and we started the game. After 2 minutes we scored our first goal but after a while the opposition started really challenging us and making it a hard game for us. At half time we knew we had to be confident to keep our 1-0 lead and win it. I was in goal for the first half and I was going to change at half time. I was upset when Mick asked me to stay in goal for the whole match. I told him that I didn't want to do it and I would play my best out field. So the coach finally agreed to that. I felt a lot of pressure on my shoulders to do well. I was thinking I have to do well or they might be annoyed with me. But I thought positively and knew I could do it. So I played well and right at the end we won 3-0. I felt very pleased and I played a great match.

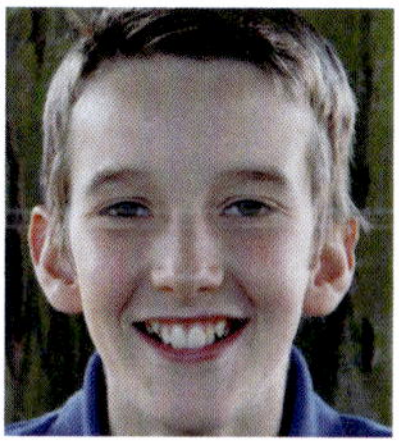

Luke, age 11

Ignore the negative & don't take things personally

When I played football, some people shouted at me when I made a mistake, like giving the ball away or missing a shot. So I had a song or positive words in my head and didn't take it personally. I listened but didn't let it get to me. Only listen to people who know what they're talking about.

Thomas B, age 11

Don't put yourself down – don't say to yourself you can't do this

If you miss an opportunity to do something, don't kick yourself, keep going. I play for Forest Academy, in a game I missed a penalty, but we still won the game. Even if some bad things do happen, good can still come.

JJ, age 11

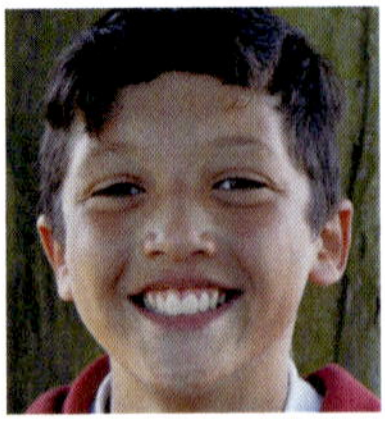

Make moving up easy

I'm moving schools in September and I may be going to a different school than my friends. I feel nervous about it but I know I'm good at making friends so I'll be ok. I feel positive about myself and know I can still get in touch with my old friends too.

Millie, age 11

ACTIVITY 2

Draw a Picture of Confident You!

How would you be standing?
How would you feel?
What would your body language be like?
Have a play and draw yourself.

When you're doing Sport

Sport is something we all do at school (and sometimes out of school too). To be good at it, it's useful to grow our confidence.

We have some ideas how:

Get back up and start again if something negative has happened

I go horse riding every week. I was in a competition at Brackenhurst. I started my round and I cleared all the fences. Then on the last one my horse got scared of the people cheering me on and I fell off and got some bruises. I decided to get back on even though it hurt and I still came 5th out of 20 riders.

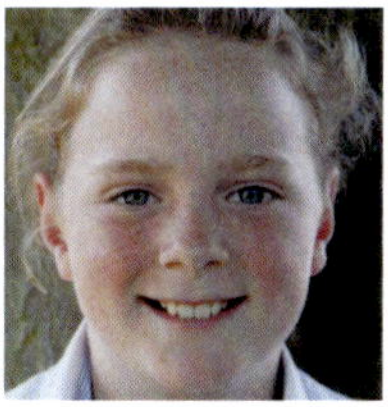

Poppy, age 10

Calm down and start again

On Thursday I went to Lambley stables and rode a pony called Rambo. I got on and followed my friend round on her pony. I went into a canter and Rambo didn't like it so he cantered into a tree. I got angry with him, and my arm was all bruised. My Mum took me into the tack room, I got a drink, calmed down and then I chose to start again. Rambo listened to me the second time and it went ok.

Millie, age 11

Do better next time

After a hard long weekend of swimming, I was tired and extremely annoyed. I had done well but I had just missed coming in the top ten in the counties. I was devastated because I missed getting into the special swimming club too!

But the next year I came back strong, doing well in all my races and in the end I came second, coming second by just one point. I was extremely pleased with myself. Finally I got into the county squad so I was very pleased!! Months after I went to a different open meet called the Midlands which was much harder. I was ready for it, my goal was to get in the top 10 and if I got that goal I would be so pleased. The event had finished, my heart was beating madly waiting for the result to come through. Finally the results came and amazingly I came 10th! Getting my goal I was so proud of myself.

Luke, age 11

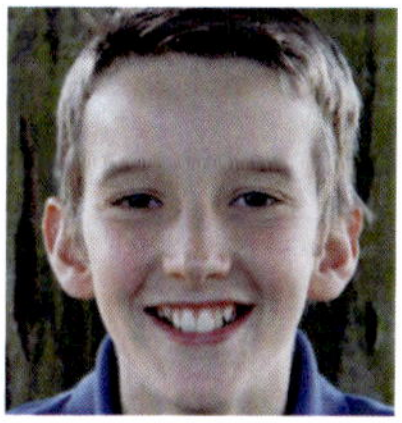

Believe in yourself, even if things don't look good

One Saturday morning, I was going to my football match against Hucknall. First I was on the sideline when we let in 2 goals. Suddenly I came on and out of the blue we scored a stunning goal. After that they scored, then it was half time. So we came back on and we got a penalty because someone handballed. Our captain took an amazing penalty. So it was 3-2 to them. Then our captain scored again so it was 3-3. Then they scored again so it was 4-3 to them. Then we scored another equaliser so it was 4-4 when it ended. So never give up, even when you start off bad. Believe in yourself.

Rio, age 10

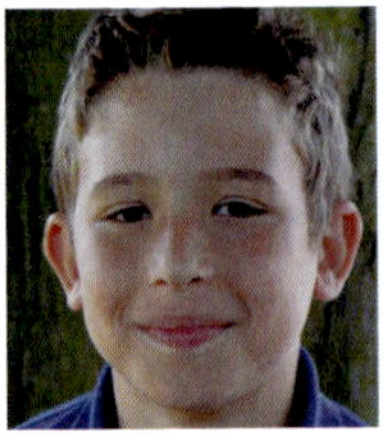

Override your negative voice inside

When I was 8 years old, I started badminton lessons. I didn't really like it to start with as there were lots of older kids hitting it really hard and showing off. I wanted to do it, but there were too many people and they were all better than me. My chatterbox was saying to me don't do it, it's too hard, everyone will laugh at you. But I still did it. I said to myself be brave, come on you can do it, and I did.

Adam, age 10

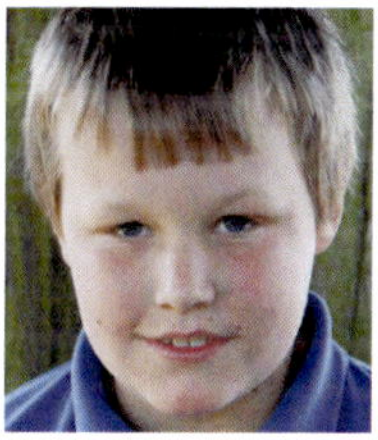

Never Give up, (even if you're behind)

I was playing in a football tournament for Hucknall Town and we were in the final and were losing 3-1. We pulled it back to 4-3 and after the game my Dad said there were loads of scouts there and you really impressed them. A couple of weeks later I got a letter saying do you want to trial for Forest Academy. So I tried out for them and then lots of academies wanted me, like Derby, Leicester, Notts County and a couple more. I now play for Forest and I really like it. Even though we were losing I didn't give up.

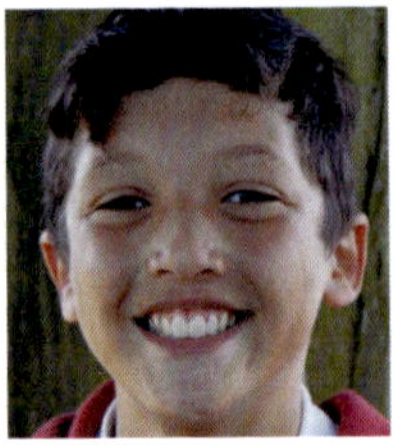

JJ, age 11

Don't listen to other people's negative opinions

What happened was, when I started playing for the school football team, everyone thought I was like a joke and I wasn't going to do very well or anything. The Manager believed I could do well and I had the potential to be very good and to play in every game of the school football team. So when people said I wasn't going to do well or even make it into the team, I just ignored them and got on. I've done really well and finally got into the school football team and I scored a goal last week when we beat Robert Mellors 8-0. I felt really proud.

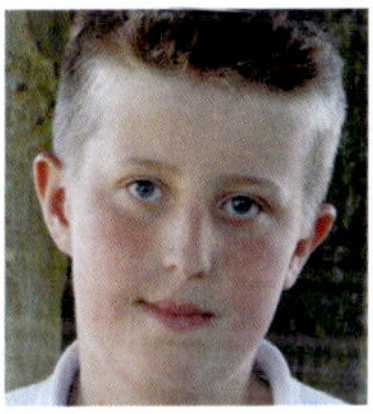

Joseph, age 11

Think of yourself in a positive, happy place

At the weekend I did a tetrathlon. At the start I was thinking I didn't want to let my team down. Sometimes I'm nervous about the shooting part because my arm shakes. But this time I felt OK and positive, I just thought I'm going to do it. I felt proud of myself because I did better than I thought I would.

Poppy, age 10

Keep thinking you're going to win

One Saturday morning I was going to a football match against Burton Joyce. We were about 5 minutes in and they got a lucky goal and all our heads went down. They got another and that made it 2-0 and we were only 15 minutes in. But suddenly we got a shot and we got a goal back and we thought we could win, but then Burton Joyce got a break and they scored again. At half time we said to ourselves we can still win this. Then we got the ball and ran and got another goal and we were back in the game at 3-2! Game on! We believed that we could win it. So then we got another goal and all the crowd got behind us and they kicked off. When we got the ball we started to pass it around and we got the ball into the box and I got fouled and so we got a penalty. I took it and I scored and it was 3-3. There was only 5 minutes left so we quickly got the ball off the opposition and hit the post and it bounced in and it was 4-3, we were about to win. When they kicked off again the whistle blew and we won! Just keep believing you're going to win.

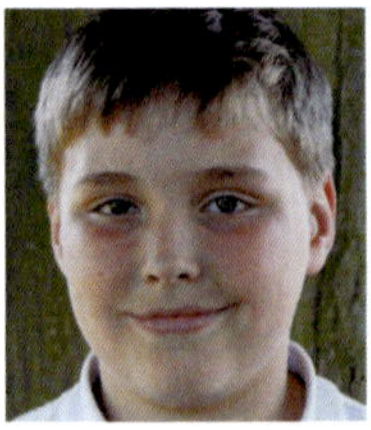

Charlie Hines, age 11

Always Do Your Best

We have sports day at school every year. It was hard and the race wasn't one of the simplest. The race was to run, pick up a skipping rope and skip through a hoop and run to the finish line. I tried my best and came in my top 3 for the first time, and that was in year three.

Henry, age 10

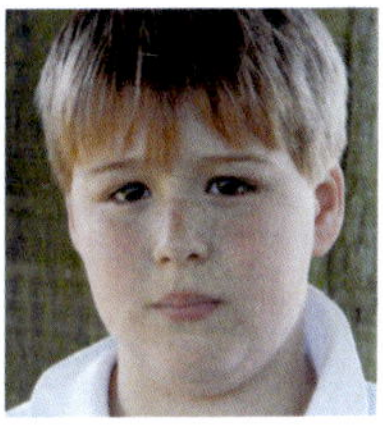

ACTIVITY 3

Ways to Be More Confident Checklist

Here's a quick checklist of how you can grow your confidence. Tick those you do already and put a star * by those you're going to do.

- ☐ Be your own best friend
- ☐ Be kind when you talk to yourself
- ☐ Compare you with you (not with other people)
- ☐ Have a go, it's much easier than you think
- ☐ Be yourself (don't try and be like someone else, you're special)
- ☐ Push through your fears; it doesn't matter what people think or say, you can do it
- ☐ Think of happy moments when you're nervous
- ☐ Ignore the negative and don't take things personally
- ☐ Be positive, expect the best
- ☐ Focus on who you are and what you're good at, not what you can't do
- ☐ When somebody says something good to you, remember it

When Something Goes Wrong

Sometimes in life, things go wrong and we can feel sad about it. We need even more confidence then and here's some ways we've done it:

Go for it, even when things don't go well to start with

I play the guitar and I've done 3 exams. On one of the exams, I didn't know I was going to do it and my mum turned up at the exam place and when I started practising I started to shake and get nervous. Then I thought, just go for it. When I came out I felt happy about what I'd done and the next week I got a letter saying that I'd got a distinction in my exam.

Syme, age 11

Do Your Best,
pick yourself up when things go wrong

I did a maths test at school and I did really badly on it. I got 4 out of 20 and I was really upset. I had to do it again and I was very annoyed with myself. I have a saying called 'positive mental attitude' abbreviated pma. So I thought to myself, come on, do your best. I took the test again and I got 19. I felt very proud of myself.

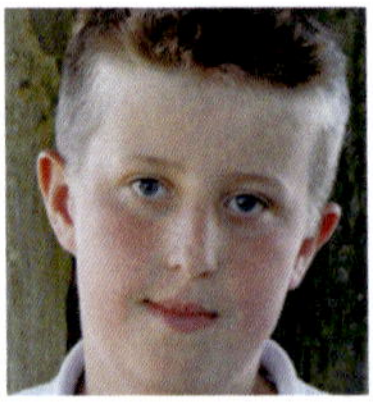

Joseph, age 11

Stand up for Yourself

I have a friend who sometimes isn't very nice to me. Sometime's he's alright and sometimes he's not. Even though he's bigger and older than me I stick up for myself. I speak firmly and say stop being mean to me or I will not go near you or speak to you again, then I turn back and walk away. That makes me feel quite happy. It's important to always stand up for yourself.

Syme, age 11

Push through your fears (don't be afraid). It doesn't matter what people think or say, you can do it

When I was at Caythorpe for my school residential, I was really scared of doing the high wire. I did want to do it but I was nervous. Luke did it and then Mrs Fossey-Taylor did it and Millie did it and she's really scared of heights. So I did the high wire in the end and I really liked it so I went round again.

Jess, age 11

Make yourself feel better

A few years back, I took street jazz lessons every week on Saturday at my Mum's work place and I felt extremely nervous. After a while, I settled in quite well and got a few of my friends from school coming as well. Every year, we did a show at the palace theatre and hundreds of people came to watch. When it was finally time for me to go up on stage with the fellow members of my group, I came on, trembling with fear. About halfway through the dance I got my timing wrong and fell behind the others, making me stand out clearly (and not in a good way). As I tried in vain to catch up with my friends, I repeatedly cursed myself for getting it wrong and, eventually, I realised that cursing myself wasn't going to help and therefore I told myself everything I could to make myself feel better about it. When I did this, it was a lot easier to keep myself in sync with the others and in the end, I finished off our dance with a BANG! So to this day, I always remember to make myself feel better about things when something goes wrong. If something is ever to go wrong, always remember to think positive and try your hardest to make yourself feel better.

Mitchell, age 11

It's ok to show your emotions

Once, in class we brought the music box in and some people were laughing because weeks before apparently I knocked over the music box and broke it. So I got a bit upset and I talked to my teacher. After that it felt better as I'd got the emotion out. Show or tell someone how you feel and you feel so much better.

Honey, age 11

Be strong, carry on when you think you can't do something

Once when I'd fallen off a horse I didn't want to get back on and then my mum said if you don't get back on you'll regret it. And so I got back on and then I nearly fell off again but I kept on trying and in the end I did it. I felt very happy and proud of myself.

Jess, age 11

Stop putting yourself down

I sometimes have had trouble with some boys at school and it's not always been easy standing up to them especially when they've said negative things. I used to go home some nights thinking badly of myself and my family kept on telling me to stop putting myself down. I have found it hard to do, but recently, I have been managing this a lot better and I have really started feeling better about myself. From this I have learnt that it is so much nicer to believe in yourself than to put yourself down.

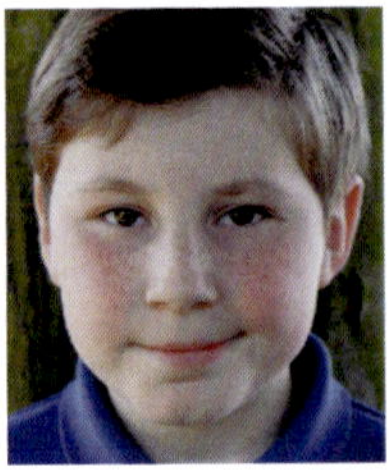

Mitchell, age 11

Put the past behind you – learn from it and move on

Last year I was swimming in a pool in South Africa when a friend called Nicholas said don't jump in. So I didn't jump in but I pushed off from the step and I heard a cracking noise. I checked my body and found that my foot was broken. When I got home I was really sad because I don't like breaking things, especially my body. I learnt from that and now every time someone says don't do that, I either don't do it or I am very careful.

Michael, age 10

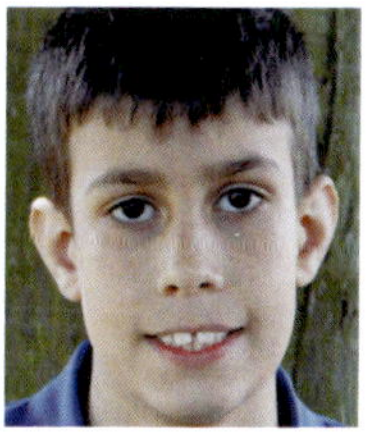

Stick with it! Don't give up at the first hurdle

I play football and we weren't doing well in my team. So I thought of moving to a new team. I found out training was on Mondays so I went to it and felt really nervous before I went. When I got there at the training ground no-one was talking to me or anything. I wondered if I'd made a mistake. They put me in the team when I went to the match on Saturday, I was playing in midfield, when I started the game no-one was passing to me. I gradually started to get the ball more and then my friend Luke turned up at a match and he was passing the ball to me and he introduced me to some of the others there. I started to make more friends. In training it started getting better and I could just talk to people. And now I'm fine, it's really good there. I'm glad I stuck with it.

Charlie, age 11

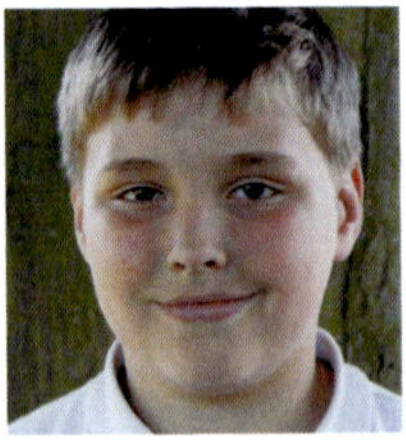

ACTIVITY 4

Draw a picture of a large tree, with strong roots. Who, what and where makes you feel safe and secure? Write in your 'who' 'where' and 'what' in the roots.

Always remember these are the roots that give you strength and security no matter what.

With Your Family

We're all different and sometimes we need to have more confidence even with our own family who we're close to.

Be Yourself. You don't have to be like your brothers & sisters

I like being myself because it's nice. I like being with my family because I can always be myself. We go out and have fun. We go to the park at Burton Joyce or go to a restaurant. I have a little sister and we get on sometimes. I never try and be like her. So Just be you.

Izaak, age 10

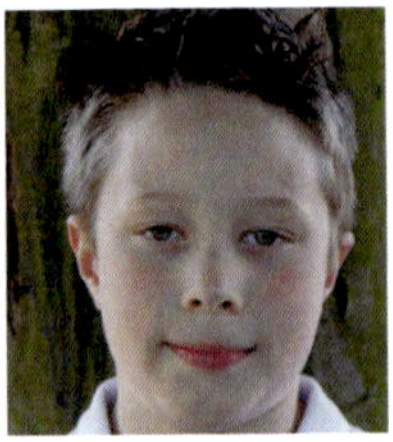

Tell your family how you really feel & what's really going on

At school me and my friends had a big argument about nothing. It was a bit upsetting because we were all arguing with each other and calling each other horrible things. When I went home, I told my mum and dad what had been going on and I told them the whole story. My dad told the head teacher and the head teacher ended up sorting the whole situation out. I learnt that I shouldn't be afraid to tell people what happens as they can always help.

Aimee, age 11

Make sure you're included and don't get left out

I have 3 little brothers and there are many incidents where one of our friends will come around and they'll be occupied with one of the younger members of the family, and so I find myself lazing around doing nothing whilst they're playing with each other. One of the times that this has happened went a bit like this; A friend came over and he was occupied playing with my nine year old brother Koby. I felt a bit upset that they were leaving me out but I didn't make a move to stop it. Eventually I'd had enough and went up to ask if I could play. They said yes immediately, and so together we played happily until my friend had to go back home and then me and Koby played with our little brother Jake and I felt a whole lot better after asking if I could play with them. So never allow anyone to leave you out, and you will be a whole lot better off.

Mitchell, age 11

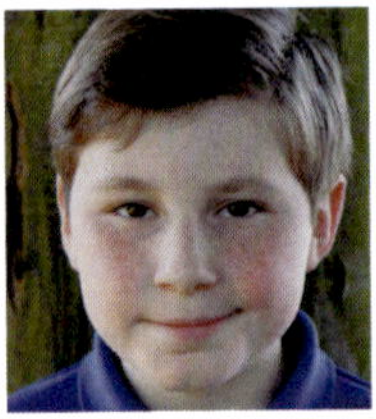

ACTIVITY 5

Who do you admire?
Who do you look up to?
Who inspires you?
Who's Your Hero/Heroine?
What is it that you like about them?
Now think about how many of those qualities you have & write them down.

You may be surprised to find more than you realise!
Keep visiting this list and adding to it!

When You're Doing Something New

When you're doing something new for the first time, it's normal to feel nervous, isn't it. Be confident and go for it.

Be yourself

I started playing tennis when I was 7. I was a bit scared of the people at the tennis lessons at first. I tried as hard as I could, I prayed and hoped that I got along with people. I didn't know the people well although now I know them and they're my friends. I get on really well with Callum & Aidan, we played matches with each other and we learnt tips from each other. And one of those tips was the spinner, where you hit the ball and kind of spin it, so the other person has to run more to stretch and get it. The instructor named Ruth was friendly and she introduced me to everyone. It made me warm inside that every single one of them was smiling. It helped a lot that I was myself, and especially that I didn't try to be someone else.

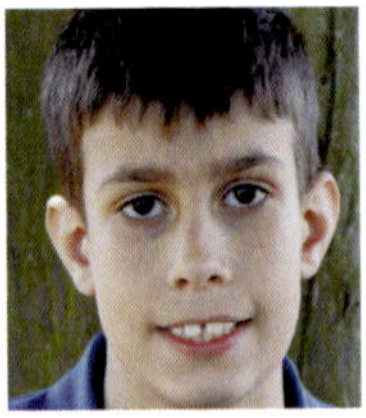

Michael, age 10

Have a go, it's much easier than you think

When I was younger, on my first day at school. I was told to write my name but I didn't think I could. I felt nervous and then the teacher told me to have a go. After some time I had a go and I did it!

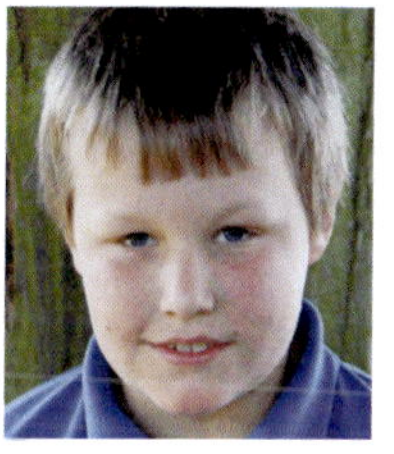

Adam, age 10

Be brave, don't panic

I went to Alton Towers with my mum and my step dad. There was a ride called Nemesis and it was really scary. I didn't know whether to go on it or not. In the end I was brave and went on the ride, and I loved it. It went really fast and did a loop the loop. If you're not sure, be brave and go for it, even if it's really scary.

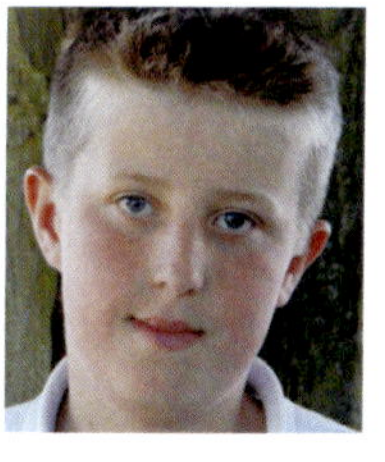

Joseph, age 11

Do your best

I joined crochet club at school and I was a bit nervous I might not be able to do the stitches. I did my best though and kept trying and in the end I managed to do the stitches and I was really proud of myself.

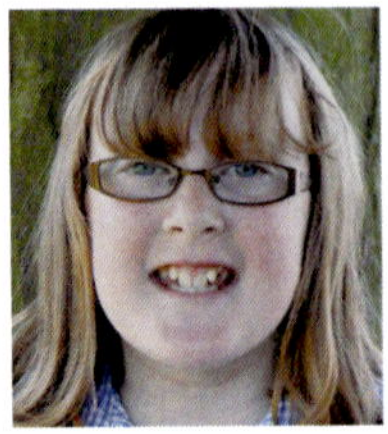

Jess, age 11

Don't worry about failure

When I was young and just started school, I was scared because I wasn't making any friends. I thought I was a failure, but right at that very second a boy named Adam said "Do you want to be friends?" I said yes and that's how I got lots of friends. He was my first best friend. Be brave, don't worry about failing!

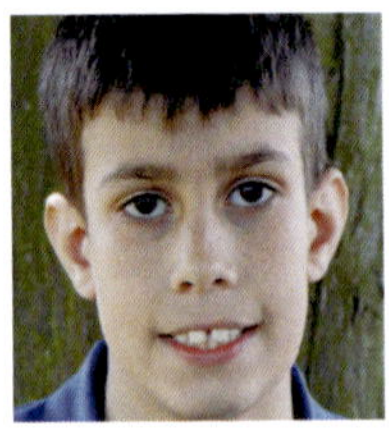

Michael, age 10

Make friends, smile and talk to people

On my first day of school I was worried that no-one would talk to me. I saw a crowd of girls all smiling and playing together. I went up to them and asked them if I could play. They said yes and we became best friends from that day.

Aimee, age 11

Talk to people who know what they're doing

I was queuing to jump off the small diving board when I was in my swimming lesson and I heard a lot of people injured themselves because of the way they dived. So I went to talk to one of the instructors and he told me to push off hard but also aim outwards and then travel downwards. So I did and I was alright.

Oliver F, age 11

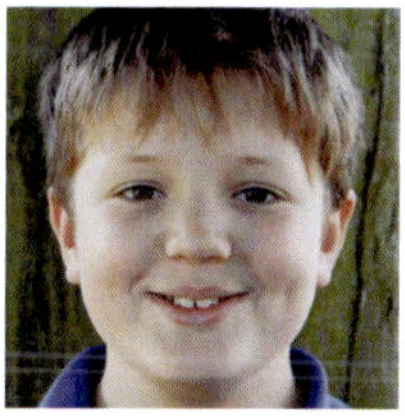

Think of positive things

When I was trying to grade for my next belt in Aikido, I felt very nervous because it was for my brown belt and I wasn't sure if I'd be able to do it. So I tried to think it doesn't matter because I can always try again and I was trying to think of what it'd mean if I did get the grade. I thought of positive things and it really helped. I kept thinking about them and the grading was finished before I knew it. I got it! I felt really good that I'd tried hard! Thinking of positive things really works.

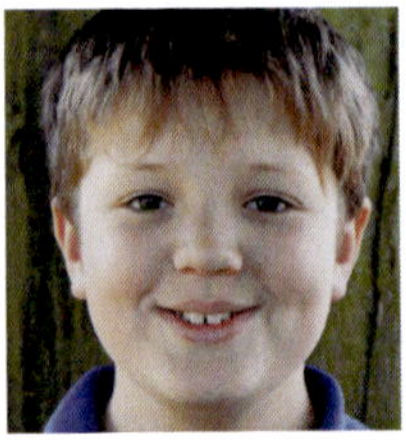

Oliver F, age 11

ACTIVITY 6

Have a go at our Confidence Wordsearch. How many of these words can you find below?

Confident	Believe	Self-Belief
Positive	Attitude	Achieve
Possible	Dreams	Best
Self-Esteem	Can	

E	F	E	I	L	E	B	-	F	L	E	S
V	Z	I	A	F	N	Q	L	S	A	K	D
E	D	H	A	C	A	N	T	E	J	X	R
I	M	H	K	O	B	O	J	V	P	E	E
L	F	S	D	N	F	E	T	I	X	V	A
E	S	E	L	F	-	E	S	T	E	E	M
B	J	E	S	I	G	H	B	I	V	I	S
C	E	G	J	D	K	O	C	S	M	H	K
F	R	S	W	E	R	G	J	O	N	C	S
E	G	H	T	N	R	Q	X	P	Z	A	N
J	P	Z	A	T	T	I	T	U	D	E	K
R	Q	P	O	S	S	I	B	L	E	K	E

With Friends

You need confidence with friends so they don't leave you out and include you in their games and you have more fun.

Talk with your friends

Once one of my friends fell out with me because I wanted to play with two of my other friends for a change. She wouldn't leave me alone and she was really annoyed because she couldn't play with me. I thought about it and a couple of minutes later I went to talk to her and said "I didn't mean to upset you" and I said "sorry but I just want to play with my other friends right now". We sorted it out. It's good to talk with your friends.

Jess, age 11

Stay clear of people who annoy you

I was playing football one day and one of my friends said something mean about me and they told other people. Then it was dinner time and one of the boys kept calling me this name. I kept out of the way and then finally I said would you please stop it and he asked what he was doing. I told him to stop telling everyone and he stopped.

Ellie, age 10

If someone makes fun of you, don't take it personally

Someone in my class kept tapping me in the middle of the back and making fun of me. I just got used to it and it doesn't bother me at all. I make a "yo momma" joke and laugh it off. If someone makes fun of you either tell your teacher or just laugh it off and don't take it personally.

Oliver I, age 10

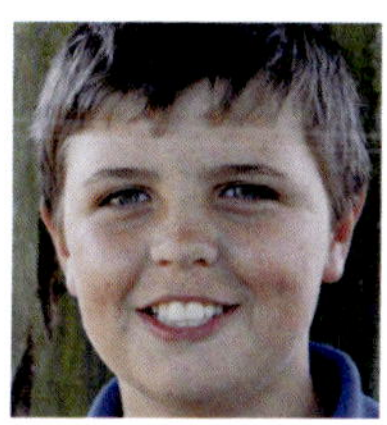

Remember you've always got you. Be a good friend to yourself

It's better to be your own best friend and your heart doesn't get broken if your best friend is mean to you. You can tell yourself secrets that won't be told by anyone else. When I started my new school in year 6, I didn't know anyone, so it helped that I was my own best friend. I think it helped me to get to know new people too.

Caitlan, age 11

ACTIVITY 7

Write a letter to yourself with your top 3 tips on being more confident and sign it. What advice would you give yourself!

Dear ....,

Fears/Phobias/ When You're Nervous

We all get nervous and are scared sometimes and it helps to know that. That it's not just you. Here are some tips for when you're feeling afraid:-

Face your fear

My sister was very scared of spiders. She would never go anywhere near them. We were sitting down at the park one day and she saw me with a spider in my hand. She ran away at first but then she asked "what is it like to hold a spider?" I said you're going to have to hold it yourself to try it out. I put it on her hand and she screamed and then she said "this is not so bad". She is now not scared of spiders. Whatever you're scared of, just face it.

Ellie, age 10

Keep moving forward in small steps to overcome your fear

When I was in the school play, all of my family were coming to see me. I felt really nervous about it. I talked to my mum and asked her what she'd do if I messed up, and she said it really wouldn't matter. I made sure I learnt the lines really well, I even skipped football! On the day I told myself not to worry and in the end I did great. I felt pleasant and glad that I'd taken a little bit of time out of my day and finally completed it. If you're nervous, speak to someone about it, it makes you feel better once you actually tell someone about your fears and don't just lock them away. Taking small steps helps too.

JJ, age 11

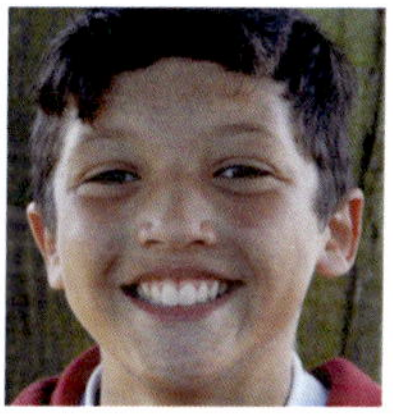

Fear just means FALSE EVIDENCE APPEARING REAL

I do kickboxing and when I did my first belt, I was super duper nervous. There's an oath my club has which is "the true meaning of fear is false evidence appearing real, impossible does not exist". This is really true and sometimes things aren't as bad as they seem.

Grace, age 10

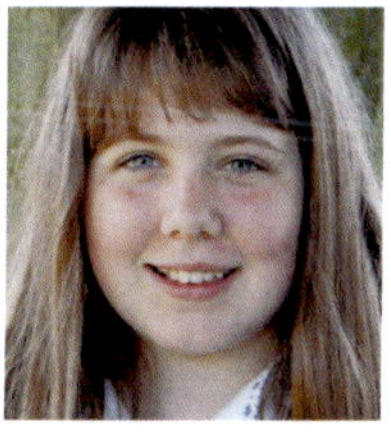

Think of happy moments when you're nervous

I used to get nervous when I was younger. There was a big boy in class 3 when I was in class 1. He used to call me names and it sometimes made me nervous to play outside and I stopped going to tuck shop because of it for a while. I played with my friends and thought about the fun we had and I felt much better. I told the teacher and she had a word with him too. Thinking about fun things helps.

Ellie, age 10

Breathing Deep Helps

If you're nervous about something, breathing deep helps you to feel more confident. When I had my first sleep over at a friend's house, I was a bit nervous as it was the first time I slept away from my mum or dad. When we went to bed it felt a bit strange and so I took some deep breathes and that helped me a lot.

Honey, age 11

ACTIVITY 8

Draw a picture of a shield with 3 items on it that represent you, showing what's important to you.

Write your motto across it. What would that be?

When you're in competitions/ Shows/Presentations

When you're in a show or competition, your heart beats quicker and you can feel nervous and excited at the same time. Have a read about what we do:

Relax – do your best

Last year me and my football team won the cup. We had to go against Ravenshead. I was very nervous. When we were in the changing rooms, I started to shake and go a bit quiet. I took 3 big breaths, and then I went out onto the football pitch and I felt a lot better because all the parents were cheering us on. Then we went on to win the cup! I felt happy. So if you're nervous take some deep breaths and just go for it.

Syme, age 11

Believe in yourself. Say I can

I was really confident with the stabilizers on my bike but then my dad decided to take them off. I was nervous when I first rode without them, but I believed in myself. I said I can do this. After I tried over and over again, I could do it. I did it! I could ride a bike without stabilisers and I still can.

Ali-Khan, age 10

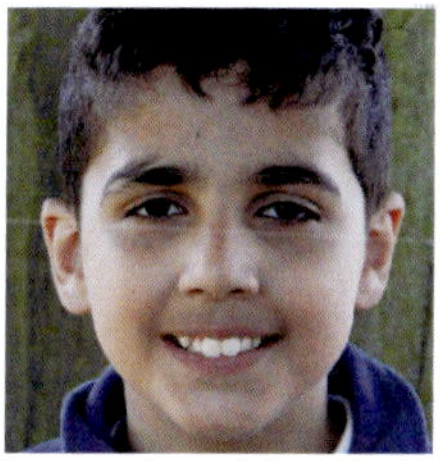

Have a go – never give up

Once when I went to Turkey, my Dad dared me to jump off a boat 6 metres tall with 3 extra feet tall steps. I was stepping up onto the top step while my heart was pounding faster than a formula 1 car. I am normally scared of deep water but I know I can swim quite well. So I just closed my eyes and jumped, I did it. It was ok, and we even saw an octopus and some sea horses. I'm happy I didn't give up.

Oliver I, age 10

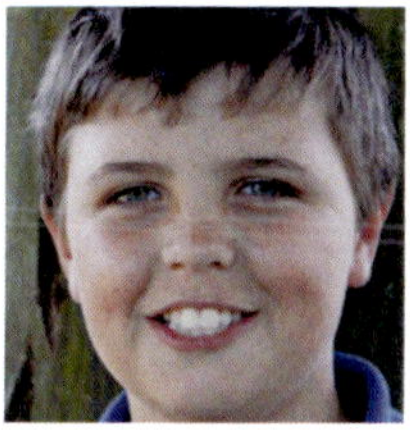

Say to yourself "I'm going to do this"

The time came, we got out of the car and walked to the grading centre. The feeling was rather pleasant and unusual. I was going to do my first kickboxing grading for my red belt and it was very nerve wracking and I was in front of the head coach so I had to do my best to succeed. I told myself I am going to do this, and I ended up getting 100 percent.

Henry, age 10

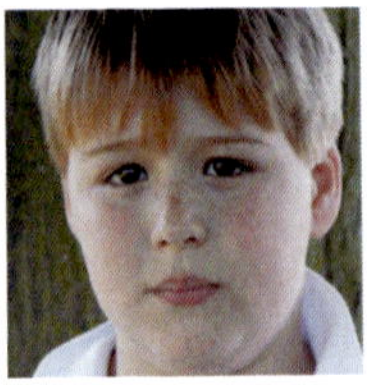

Just do it. What is the worst that can happen?

On my first grading for Fencing, I was a bit worried when it got to one move, a parry kart, and I thought I was never going to be able to do it. I started to get sweaty inside the mask. Our coach is really strict, he used to be in the army, so I thought he would get annoyed with me. When he said "go", he did a lunge at me and I just did it. I thought, what's the worst that can happen here, and had a go! And I passed my grading!

Oliver B, age 10

Be happy

There was a talent competition at school for red nose day. Me and a friend thought we should do a dance to Gangnam Style. Another friend joined us and we changed the music to I'm Sexy & I Know It. We went dressed all in red. When we were practising it was funny and my friend kept messing around, he couldn't stand up properly. He kept forgetting the moves, and on the day he wasn't doing any better. On the day itself we hadn't had much practise and were nervous but decided just to have fun. We stood up and did it and everyone loved it and they were all clapping even those in our competition. Everyone was laughing their heads off.

Ali-Khan, age 10

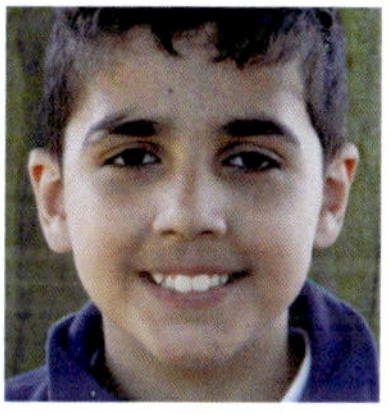

I joined the dance and what happened was that my friend started to laugh at everything that I did. He said on the day it'd be fine and he wouldn't mess around. On the day itself, he was still messing around. When we did it, it was awesome and everyone was laughing, even the teachers. So just go for it and be happy.

Oliver B, age 10

Don't be worried. Don't stress. Go with the flow

I was in a street dance crew with some of my friends and we had entered a competition where there were a few auditions, totally different. Some of them were singing, some of them were just dancing, some were doing ballet. But we were doing street dancing and we had been practising and preparing ourselves for this day. I was so happy the whole time we were practising but when it came to the day, I was a bit nervous because I didn't want to mess it up for my crew. So I tried to have a smile on my face, mixing with the people and trying to forget about the dance. When I went up to my friends and saw them all laughing together it made me feel happier so I went along with them and kept my cool and didn't get all emotional even though there was hundreds of people standing in the crowd. But then we went on and as soon as we started dancing it felt like I was alive. By the time we had finished it went so quick and I loved it so much that I wanted to do it again. All the crowd was cheering us on and I felt really amazing. So keep calm and don't think too much.

Rio, age 10

ACTIVITY 9

What makes you happy?
Where do you love to be?
What do you love to do?
Where do you love to go?
Write a list as long as you can.

TIP: Keep this list & look at it often. If you're feeling low it can help you feel much better.

Here's What Others Say about Self-Belief & Confidence!

We asked some people who are highly respected in their professions, some of them household names, to share their tips with you on what they wish they'd known when they were 10 years old, about the importance of self belief and confidence.

Here's what Richard Branson, Stuart Pearce, Prime Minister's Office, Sian Williams, Rory Delap, Kerensa Jennings, Billy Schwer, David Wood, Emma Clayton, Gareth Evans, Gary Bailey, have to say:

Richard Branson

What advice would you give to a 10 year old about the importance of believing in themselves?

"When I was four, my mum stopped the car and dropped me off at the side of the road and made me find my own way home. Of course I got lost but I kept walking and finally ended up at a house, which turned out to be a neighbour's. I was gone long enough that my mum ended up quite worried but it was a good lesson in not to be afraid and trust my instincts. That is never more true when you're faced with doing nothing or doing the right thing. Have you seen a friend get picked on or teased by other kids? Do you walk away or do you stick up for them? Do you dream of inventing something that no one has yet seen? You have the ability to change the world and make it better for yourself and others. Once you have made a difference, you will go on to do it again and again because what once seemed impossible will feel like the only path, the better path, to pursue. And that all starts with believing in yourself."

Richard Branson is the founder of the Virgin empire, entrepreneur and philanthropist.

The Prime Minister's Office,
10 Downing Street

What advice would you give a 10 year old about the importance of self belief and confidence?

"The children of today are the future of our country – our future doctors, nurses, engineers, scientists, sports stars, politicians –even Prime Ministers! The key to unlocking this future is believing in yourself, and those around you. With hard work, and this self-assurance, who knows what might one day be possible."

The Prime Minister's Office, 10 Downing Street

Stuart Pearce

What advice would you give a 10 year old about the importance of self belief and confidence?

"The importance of self belief is paramount because if you have that belief in yourself then it radiates out to others and affects the way they treat you, it's a sort of mirror image. That belief and self worth comes from you and is so important at your age. Probably those around you can enhance your self belief in the things they say and do; your parents, your friends, and others. But it's really important that the inner self belief and confidence emanates from you to others and is so key to the way they treat you. Everyone gets knock backs in life in one way shape or form. I've certainly had my fair share of them in my life, rejected by football clubs, told I wasn't good enough, that sort of thing. You have to have that self belief within you to go out and prove people wrong."

Stuart Pearce, Nottingham Forest Legend. Former Forest and England Captain & former England U21 Manager

Sian Williams,

Radio/TV Presenter

What advice would you give your 10 year old self about confidence and self belief?

"I was a small, skinny girl and always the last to be picked for team games. I struggled to fit into any of the groups - I wasn't in the "popular" crowd, or the "sporty" crowd, so was left to get on with my own thing. Some of the kids could be a bit nasty, because I was different and I was bullied for a while. I was good at reading and writing, though. One day, I was asked to produce the school play. I picked people who were always on the outside, who were never picked for anything. The lead character was given to a boy called Simon, who sometimes had problems speaking. He was so enthusiastic and so brilliant at the part, that others looked differently at him. That's when I realised, it doesn't matter what group you are in, it doesn't matter if you can't play sports, or you don't have the latest fashions, or you are somehow, different to others. You have a part to play. When you look back, as an adult, you'll be glad you held your head up high, stayed different and supported others who felt excluded."

Sian Williams, BBC Radio/TV Presenter, currently presenting on Saturday Live

Kerensa Jennings,

Award winning producer/director, BBC

What advice would you give your 10 year old self about self belief and confidence?

"If I could go back and talk to the Ten Year Old Me, I'd ask her to try to believe in her story-telling, because in future it wouldn't be her scribbles on the price of commodities that would interest people, but her ability to tell stories and her love of helping others.

I'd encourage her to keep writing and to keep practising, pretending to make TV programmes because one day it would all pay off and she would become a real producer and director and get to makeprogrammes on dinosaurs with Sir David Attenborough.

On the days when she felt a bit sad because some of the other children at school were cruel (a particularly bad day was when Ten Year Old Me got locked up in the broom cupboard next to the assembly hall by a pair of bullies) – I would tell her to be strong and kind, no matter what. Being true to who she was at the very core of her being – that's what matters. Sometimes people can be a bit rubbish and treat you badly. Ten Year Old Me shed a fair few tears back then. But I'd tell Ten Year Old Me to trust her instincts and to treat others how she would want to be treated. These days I am a qualified Executive Coach as well as a producer/director who's worked with some of the most famous people in the world– Royalty, sporting heroes, pop stars and politicians. I've filmed everywhere from inside Buckingham Palace, to the middle of a refugee camp; deep within a coal mine to abseiling down a mountain on a dinosaur dig and navigating an exploding quarry.

So Ten Year Old Me – hang in there, let your difficult experiences help make you who you are. You turn out ok."

Kerensa Jennings is Producer/Director and Executive Coach for the BBC, who's worked on programmes like Fossil Detectives with Sir David Attenborough and Breakfast with Frost with Sir David Frost.

Billy Schwer,
Former World Boxing Champion

What advice would you give a 10 year old about self belief and confidence?

"Belief will give you the courage, heart and spirit to become world class. I became a world boxing champion and I was just like you, normal. From when I was 13 years of age I realised if I could find the courage to step up, put myself at risk, even be prepared to fail I could succeed. I became a national champion at 13 because I overcame my fear of failure. I believed I could do it, I was so nervous and frightened that I actually threw up before the contest. My belief is what made me succeed in the face of fear and failure. If I can do it you can too..."

Billy Schwer is now a Mental Fitness Professional Speaker & Professional Coach

Rory Delap,
Professional Footballer

What advice would you give your 10 year old self about confidence and self belief?

"I think that self belief is the most important factor in achieving your aim or goal and you have to be mentally strong not listen to people who tell you you can't do, achieve or become whatever you dream of being."

Rory Delap has played for Ireland, Derby County, Stoke City

Gary Bailey

What advice would you give a 10 year old about the importance of self belief and confidence?

"When I was about 15, my teacher told the class that only 2 or 3 of a class of 25 would ever get degrees at university and that the rest of us would never achieve anything impressive... as I was in the middle of the class with my results, I nearly didn't take the test to do the advanced maths for those who felt they might need it in order to go to university... I thought 'what chance did I have?' but I would rather try and fail than not try at all. I passed which gave me confidence and went on to complete my degree at university, while playing for Man Utd... so don't let anybody tell you what you can't do... rather try to achieve your dreams and if you can't reach them, then at least you tried your best!"

Gary Bailey was a professional footballer, playing for Manchester United amongst other teams

Emma Clayton

What advice would you give a 10 year old about the importance of self belief and confidence?

"When I was ten years old I had a hobby, which was dancing. Every night of the week, after school and all day Saturday's, I would beat dancing doing ballet, tap, modern and disco. My Mum ran a dancing school and thought that instead of me hanging round the streets after school it would be much better for me to be doing something constructive. Mum could also keep an eye on me at the same time! I would often have the 'mick' taken out of me from other kids at school for always going to dance class and for apparently having a 'posh' accent. Dancing was something that I grew to have a huge love and passion for. Sometimes I struggled academically at school but I soon started to find that my hobby was helping me feel more confident and have self belief as a person both at school and in life in general.

My hobby turned into my career and at the age of 18 I became a Professional Dancer which then led onto becoming a Choreographer and Movement Director. My 'Posh' accent has also led me onto having a career as an actress both in theatre and T.V. when I'm not dancing, directing or choreographing. With Choreography I work on a lot in Children's Theatre; shows such as The Tiger Who Came To Tea, Alien's Love Underpants, The Witches, Fantastic Mr Fox, *to name but a few, hopefully, encouraging children to enjoy the World of Theatre and maybe inspire them to have both a passion for seeing theatre and for maybe in the future actively taking part. It has given me so much pleasure in life doing what I do that I hope I can inspire others in enjoying my work as much as I do. Doing your hobby for a living is pretty cool! Remember with self belief, anything's possible."*

Emma Clayton is a Director/Choreographer/Actress

David Wood

What advice would you give a 10 year old about the importance of self belief and confidence?

"When I was 10, I persuaded two friends to help me put on some puppet plays I had written. We performed them in the garden for other children and raised money for charity. Nearly sixty years later I'm still writing plays and putting them on! I was lucky, because from an early age I knew what I wanted to do– to entertain and work in the theatre. Really wanting to do something and believing I could do it must have given me confidence. My advice to young people is to try lots of things, experience different sports and arts and crafts, go to concerts, zoos, libraries, museums, find out about science, how things work, politics, world problems, join in things, volunteer to help, learn to play a musical instrument, swim, act, take photos, paint a picture, make a model, read books... suck it and see. You won't enjoy everything. You won't be good at everything. But you stand a good chance of finding something you enjoy, something you can do well, something you might want to learn more and more about and make part of yourlife or make your job in the future. And you will have discovered self-belief.

My advice to teachers and parents is to give your young people the chance and the encouragement to experiment, to experience and to have a go at lots of different activities, to help them find that special interest that can change their lives."

David Wood, OBE, is a Playwright, Children's Author, Theatre & TV Producer & Director, and an Actor

Gareth Evans,
Radio Presenter

What advice would you give a 10 year old about the importance of believing in themselves?

"YOU CAN do ANYTHING that's already being done by other people, the fact that someone is reading the news on the telly, scoring the winning goal for Forest, packing out Nottingham Arena means it is possible. That someone was, at some point, where you are at now. Believing you can do it takes no more energy than believing you can't – and it is so much more fun."

Gareth Evans, Radio Presenter

About Lambley Primary School

Lambley Primary School is set in the village of Lambley in the heart of Nottinghamshire. Our strap line is "Learning is Fun", something the school prides itself on. Here's what the Head Teacher says about the school:

A Special Place to be...

We think that Lambley Primary School is a very special place to be. Our aim is to provide the very highest standards of education within a caring, exciting and stimulating environment. We believe in challenging our children, to help them achieve their full potential. We are committed to ensuring that all of our pupils are excited by the curriculum. We want them to enjoy their learning and feel valued. By working closely with parents we ensure that all our children have an excellent start to their education.

Every Child is Unique

At Lambley we make sure we know each child really well. We want to ensure that everyone enjoys school and feels safe and secure. We place great importance on fostering all aspects of each child's development: social, emotional, physical, moral and cultural as well as academic.

From Reception through to Year 6, the children's self respect, confidence and ability to work both independently and cooperatively is positively promoted. We teach our children to have self-discipline and a sense of responsibility for their own well-being and for that of other people and the environment.
We are part of the national Healthy Schools Initiative and actively encourage children to promote a healthy lifestyle. Children have lots of opportunities to take part in sport and develop healthy minds and bodies. Our school meals are cooked on the premises and provide balanced meals to high nutritional standards. Children learn about balanced diet both through science and P.E. lessons. We make sure that the children have access to fruit and water throughout the day.

We genuinely care about each and every child and want to give them the best possible start in their education and lifelong learning adventure.

To find out more about us visit:

www.lambleyprimaryschool.org.uk

About The ChildLine Schools Service

Protecting a Generation

The ChildLine Schools Service is a ground-breaking service that aims to visit all primary schools in the UK once every two years to talk to children about abuse, how to protect themselves and where to get help if they need it.

Through age appropriate assemblies and workshops, specially trained volunteers help children to understand abuse in all its forms - including bullying. By giving children the knowledge and confidence to speak out we hope to start a societal change that will bring about a long term reduction in child cruelty.

The Now I Know appeal supports the ChildLine Schools Service by raising vital funds to recruit and train local volunteers. The appeal aims to raise £20 million to ensure that children can say 'Now I know' and not 'I wish I had known'.

ChildLine:
0800 1111
www.childline.org.uk

ChildLine, which is a service provided by the NSPCC, is the UK's free, confidential 24-hour service for children and young people who need to talk, whatever their worry. Trained counsellors provide advice and support over the phone and online.

About Michael Wisher Our Sponsor

Business owner and philanthropist Michael Wisher is one of Nottingham's busiest entrepreneurs. He is Director of hospitality recruitment agency Michael Wisher & Assoc, Director of Nottingham Motor Co, an Ambassador of New College Nottingham and a Partner with English Homes Estate Agents.

As a classic car enthusiast, Michael uses his personal resources to support the national children's charity Sporting Bears, and sponsors events in aid of Help a Nottinghamshire Child.

About Lisa Spencer-Arnell

Lisa Spencer-Arnell is mum to Grace & Jack and is passionate about **people** (loves spending time with family and her work developing leaders), **football** (a Nottingham Forest fan!) and **the next generation**, (she'd love all children to have great self esteem and really believe in themselves). She's one of the authors of *Emotional Intelligence Coaching* & *Who Stole My Success.*

To contact Lisa,
visit: www.lisaspencerarnell.com
or email: lisa@ccs-coaching.co.uk

And finally, here's Lisa's tip:

"Be who you are, believe in yourself & know that anything's possible!"

To help grow your confidence, here's a great little affirmation that my friend Jackie Wilson shares at her children's yoga sessions and confidence workshops for kids:-

I am Special
I am Important
Not Because of What I Look Like
Not Because of What I Wear
Not Because of What I Have
But Because I am!

Thank You!

We hope you've enjoyed reading our book and found our tips useful. Please tell your friends and ask them to help us change the world, by helping other kids and raising money for a great charity.

Our website is:

www.confidenceforkidsbykids.com